# THE

## *Quick*

## &

## DIRTY

# HANDBOOK

# THE Quick & DIRTY HANDBOOK

*JUST MAKE IT QUICK & DIRTY*

## BY G. ROBERT MICHAELIS

Writer's Showcase

San Jose  New York  Lincoln  Shanghai

**The "Quick and Dirty" Official Quick and Dirty Handbook**

Writer's Showcase
an imprint of iUniverse.com, Inc.

For information address:
iUniverse.com, Inc.
5220 S 16th, Ste. 200
Lincoln, NE 68512
www.iuniverse.com

ISBN: 0-595-13899-3

Printed in the United States of America

# Dedication

My utmost thanks and appreciation go to Mr. Mark Balderson and Mr. Hak-chul Chung (deceased) for being "quick & dirty" mentors. They were consummate business professionals whose work I highly respected, and they truly were gifted in being able to do things "quick & dirty". Under constant bombardment with "quick & dirty" requirements necessitating "quick & dirty" solutions, they continually exceeded every demand, while maintaining their sanity, due in large pert to their abundant senses of humor, a necessary trait for those who have to do things "quick & dirty". I also want to thank my brother in law Gary Rufner, who critiqued my work and who lent his support for writing this book.

A special thanks also goes to my wife, Karen, who never does anything "quick & dirty". Well, there have been a few leftover dinners that could be classified as having been done "quick & dirty". Nevertheless, she is very thorough, neat and clean in everything she does.

# Contents

# Introduction

This book was written as an exercise in doing thinsg "quick & dirty". You will find misspellings and grammatical errors throughout the book, keeping in form with its intent, which is a book on "quick & dirty" done "quick & dirty". In all, it took approximately five or six hours of writing and one hour to put it all together, qualifying this as truly a "quick & dirty" work. I intended the book to be universally used used by any business in any field, large, or small. Employees need to know both how and when to do things "quick & dirty". This book should be made required reading. Human Resources should have a half dozen or more copies on hand, especially for new hires. Project managers, if not each employee, should also have a copy to use for reference and as an example of what is expected when something is to be done "quick & dirty". It is hoped that you find the book amusing, yet briefly accurate and marginally informative. There is no doubt in my mind that you will be required to do something "quick & dirty" at some point in your career. This book should help you be successful in doing or avoiding doing things "quick & dirty".

# Quick & Dirty History

Quick & Dirty has its origins when things were first created, no matter your religious or scientific beliefs. Big Bang, that qualifies as "quick and dirty". God created heaven and earth in about a week How's that for "quick & dirty"? How about the caveman? He used the "quick and dirty" approach in courtship. He clubbed his soon-to-be mate over the head didn't he?

There have been "quick & dirty" wars, the Gulf War and the Arab-Israel War. There have been "quick & dirty" shotgun marriages. "Quick & Dirty" has been prevalent in computer applications to help us do our work. This is more formally known as Rapid Application Development (RAD).

Far and away the most infamous "quick & dirty" usage comes from the computer industry. The following is from Encarta:

In 1979 Gates and Allen moved the company to Bellevue, Washington, a suburb of their hometown of Seattle. (The company moved to its current headquarters in Redmond in 1986.) In 1980 International Business Machines Corporation (IBM) chose Microsoft to write the operating system for the IBM PC personal computer, to be introduced the following year. Under time pressure, Microsoft purchased QDOS (**Quick and Dirty** Operating System) from Seattle programmer Tim Paterson for $50,000 and renamed it MS-DOS (Microsoft Disk Operating System). As part of its contract with IBM, Microsoft was permitted to license the operating system to other companies. By 1984 Microsoft had licensed

MS-DOS to 200 personal computer manufacturers, making MS-DOS the standard operating system for personal computers and driving Microsoft's enormous growth in the 1980s.[1]

How's that for a "quick & dirty" success story?

---

1. "Microsoft Corporation," Microsoft® Encarta® Encyclopedia 2000. © 1993-1999 Microsoft Corporation. All rights reserved.

# Quick & Dirty Defined

Quick & Dirty is both an approach and a philosophy on how to get things accomplished when there is insufficient time to do a thorough and refined job.

Doing things "quick & dirty" is neither a science nor an art. Businaphorically ( a keen new word meaning business process related ) it's a "**FART**", a "Fundamental Activity Reduction Technique".

Any activity usually involves preparation, doing, and cleanup. "Quick & Dirty" eliminates the preparation and cleanup, leaving only doing. Nike's original slogan was the essence of "quick & dirty" "just do it".

There are a coup[le of "Quick and Dirty" web sites: **Quick and Dirty Guide to Image Maps** and **Quick Dirty Scrawly.** Probably there will be more soon after this book becomes highly read.

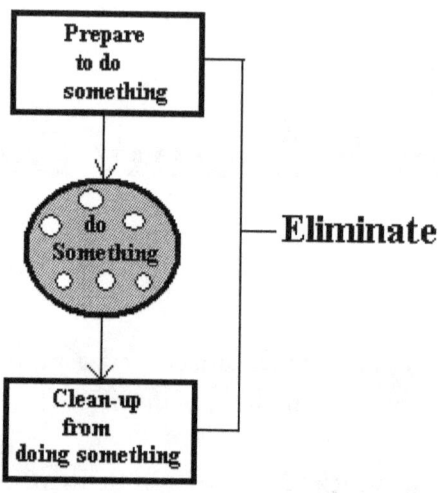

Quick & Dirty Diagram

The above diagram shows the process of "Quick & Dirty". Note that the center figure is a circle with holes in it. This is because in doing "quick & dirty" you cut all corners and there are things that are left out.

The essence of "quick & dirty" is "doing".

Note also that there is no caption. They are unnecessary time consumers in "Q & D".

# Identify your work as having been done "Quick & Dirty"

If you do not want to get into trouble with your boss, you should let him know that your work was done "quick & dirty". It is strongly suggested that you turn in any written work with a subheading of "A Quick & Dirty Work", even though it will be obvious from the outset that the work was done "quick & dirty". In defense, you really should have a signed agreement that your work was acceptable if done "quick & dirty".

*BUZZZZZZZ—Quick Violation*

## Whoa! No reviewing. Not with "quick & dirty".

Reviewing is necessary for a thorough understanding of most any project, but since you are only interested in becoming familiar enough to do the job, reviewing is unnecessary. In fact you should avoid anything that has a "re" in front of it.

*BUZZZZZZZ—Quick Violation*

## Whoa! No analyzing. Not with "quick & dirty".

You probably heard of the expression "paralysis by analysis". This no doubt was coined by someone in the heat of "quick & dirty", who was temporarily disabled by consideraing too many things.

*BUZZZZZZZ—Dirty Violation*

## Whoa! No cleaning-up. Not with "quick & dirty".

Many people like to clean up things as they go along, saving them from a huge end-of-job clean up. Well, you can't do that because all of your efforts have to be directed toward getting the job done quickly. Don't mess with mess.

*BUZZZZZZZ—Quick/Dirty Violation*

## Whoa! No organizing. Not with "quick & dirty".

By the time you get all your ducks in a row, there may be next to no time left, so simply have at it.

*BUZZZZZZZ—Quick Violation*

## Whoa! No straightening. Not with "quick & dirty".

You can straighten things out only when finished. Things are best left where they are. By the time you get things straightened out, you are likely to be out of time, and maybe out of a job. Neat freaks have great difficulty with doing things quick & dirty. Avoid them.

*BUZZZZZZZ—Quick Violation*

## Whoa! No refining Not with "quick & dirty".

Refining takes too much time and energy. You are not creating a masterpiece, just a thumbnail sketch.

*BUZZZZZZZ—Quick Violation*

## Whoa! No thinking. Not with "quick & dirty".

Thinking may cause deep concentration and maybe even isolation, which only causes a delay in doing. "I don't think, I just do" was told to me by a Q&D Master.

*BUZZZZZZZ—Quick Violation*

## Whoa! No pausing. Not with "quick & dirty".

You are in a sprint with no breaks permitted. Put on your track shoes. Drop the hammer.

*BUZZZZZZZ—Quick Violation*

## Whoa! No ordering. Not with "quick & dirty".

It matters very little what order things are done in when doing things "quick & dirty", but since you do not want to do things over, you had better have a good idea at the outset what order will get you there the fastest. This should probably be No re-ordering, but I would have to redo this, which is an assumed "quick & dirty" violation.

*BUZZZZZZZ—Quick Violation*

## Whoa! No elaborating. Not with "quick & dirty".

Elaboration is for projects where there are no time constraints. You are only interested in the minimal facts and observations when discussing things "quick & dirty".

# Do's

To be sure, there are many more "don'ts" than "do's ", but there are four primary ones: approximate, abbreviate, paraphrase, and assume.

# Abbreviate

You can convey the same amt. of info when abbrv, saving time and resources. Abbrv is a necessary part of "Q & D".

# Paraphrase

Paraphrasing generally takes less time and words, but conveys the same thing. It's a must when doing "quick & dirty".

# Assume

The more you assume, the more time you can save. "Quick and Dirty" by its very nature is ripe with assumptions. These assumptions are best not written down because they may be taken into question, causing significant delay. It is assumed that you know all of the things that have been left out of this book.

# Approximate

If acceptable (it should be strongly suggested) approximate as much and as often as you can. It can save loads of time and since you already got the go-ahead to do something "quick & dirty", you need to just be close.

# Best Time

Withoput a doubt, Fridays are the best days to do something "quick & dirty". There are fewer people around to get in your way because Friday is the highest absentee day of the workweek. Afternoons on Fridays are ideal especially when it is due by COB Friday. "Quick & Dirty" is not just the approach of choice. It is the only choice. Relax, in all likelihood, anything that was done on Friday, won't be evaluated until late Monday or Tuesday anyway. It is generally expected that things done on Fridays will have to be redone anyway. You should never buy a car that was manufactured on Friday, neither a suit, nor anything else where you want top quality. Fridays are in essence the beginning of preparing for the weekend. It may as well be considered a weekend day. Golf courses already know this, because they charge weekend rates on Fridays. I'm personally for a four day workweek with Friday beign a bona-fide

weekend day. I think we should all have a sick out on Fridays for the month of November of 2000 to let the soon to be new president of the US know what his first act as president should be - Fridays off. Talk about starting out with the highest popularity of any president. "Mr. President, two is too few...you should agree with 3". Nasty Friday rush hour commutes home will be a thing of the past. Of course, there will be those who will be tempted to go for 4 days off beginning with Thursday. Shouldn't we be though. Think of the pace for those three days. After all, we are getting a lot more done in less time with faster computers and all. Alas, the sad reality is that we probably will never see a standard 4 day workweek, even if it would improve mental & physical health, not to mention morale.

# Quick & Dirty Fitness

Doing things "quick & dirty" does require a certain level of stamina. If you are out of shape, you could seriously injure yourself when doing something quick & dirty. To get in shape it is recommended that you practice fast walking, fast talking, and fast typing/writing four or five times a week for a period of 20 to 30 minutes at a time for a minimum of about two weeks. Also, performing the following "quick & dirty" exercises will help get you in "quick & dirty" shape.

> Take five quick, short steps forward. Do not turn. Take five quick short steps backward. Do this enough times to increase your heart rate to 20 beats faster than is your norm. Continue this forward and backward stepping for about ten minutes in preparation for your other exercises. Be sure to do this in different places if you don't want to wear a rut in the carpeting. It is better however to do it on hard flooring for better traction.
> Say the following sentence as fast as you can.

"I will say things as fast as I can, abbreviating and paraphrasing as often as I can."

**You need only say it once to set the pace at which you will say things when doing things "quick & dirty."**

**Write the following sentence as if your pen were on fire. I will write things as fast as I can without concern for spelling, punctuation or grammar**

You should also develop the following characteristics

Fast thinker—pondering or reflecting will only slow you down
Fast reflexes—cat-like reflexes will save you lots of time
Total recall—you need to try to know everything anout everything
Thick skinned—you need to be unconcerned with a lot of likely criticism

# "Quick & Dirty" Products, Businesses & Pursuits

There are several books available from the public library with "quick & dirty" in their titles. The following are examples of products, businesses and pursuits that have evolved out of a need to do things "quick & dirty". Of course, there are numerous other examples, but in keeping with the "quick & dirty" write-up of this book, these will suffice.

## Microwave oven

The microwave oven is the Q & D way to cook. Just throw a dish in there and you can have a meal in no time.

Microwaves cook food rapidly and efficiently because, unlike conventional ovens, they heat only the food and not the air or the oven walls. The heat spreads within food by conduction (*see* Heat Transfer). Microwave ovens tend to cook moist food more quickly than dry foods, because there is more water to absorb the microwaves. However, microwaves cannot penetrate deeply into foods, sometimes making it difficult to cook thicker foods.[2]

---

2. "Microwave Oven," Microsoft® Encarta® Encyclopedia 2000. © 1993-1999 Microsoft Corporation. All rights reserved.

# Gattling gun

The first Q & D way to mow down a lot of people at once was the gattling gun.

Developed during the American Civil War (1861-1865) as the first practical machine gun, the Gatling gun initially fired 350 rounds of ammunition a minute. Later versions of the gun fired 1200 rounds a minute. The Gatling gun was primarily used on the American frontier in the 1880s and in the Spanish-American War (1898).[3]

---

3. "Gatling Gun," Microsoft® Encarta® Encyclopedia 2000. © 1993-1999 Microsoft Corporation. All rights reserved.

# Shareware

There are a lot of Q & D applications available from shareware. You might want to visit the web site shareware.com. PK Zip initially was a neat little Q & D shareware product for compressing files and is widely used today. Using Windows NT, you can right click on a file and zip it right from Windows NT Explorer.

**Shareware,** in computer science, copyrighted computer software that is distributed free of charge but is usually accompanied by a request for a small payment from satisfied users to cover costs and registration for documentation and program updates.[4]

## Anabolic Steroids

The Q & D way to gain muscle mass is with anabolic steroids.

Anabolic steroids induce weight gain and increased muscle mass. Originally developed to help cancer patients and victims of starvation,

---

4. "Shareware," Microsoft® Encarta® Encyclopedia 2000. © 1993-1999 Microsoft Corporation. All rights reserved.
5. "Steroids," Microsoft® Encarta® Encyclopedia 2000. © 1993-1999 Microsoft Corporation. All rights reserved.

they are derived from the male sex hormone testosterone. In recent decades steroids have been abused by many athletes hoping to improve performance. Besides the unfairness their use introduces into competition, steroids can have serious psychological and physiological side effects, including increased aggressive behavior and cancer of the liver. The International Olympics Committee banned the use of steroids in 1974, after gas chromatography testing for their presence became possible. A number of athletes have been disqualified in competitions.[5]

# Lobotomy

Certainly there is no place for "quick & dirty" in brain surgery. Wrong!

Having heard about an Italian who had developed a trans-orbital approach to the frontal lobe (i.e., by inserting a leucotome after making an opening in the roof of the eye orbits), he invented in 1945 a much quicker and simpler way: the so-called "**ice-pick lobotomy**". Instead of a leucotome, which required a surgical trepanning, he used a common tool to break ice, which could be inserted under local anesthesia by tapping it with a hammer. The ice pick would perforate skin, subcutaneous tissue, bone and meninges in a single plunge; and then Freeman would swing it to severe the prefrontal lobe. This would take no more than a few minutes, with no need to intern the patient in the hospital.

How's that for "quick and dirty" brain surgery.

## ICE PICK LOBOTOMY

# Plea bargain

The Q & D method used to settle cases is the plea-bargain. It is widely used in criminal cases where there are too many cases with too little time to go through long drawn-out proceedings

Main Entry: **plea bargaining**

Function: *noun*

Date: 1964

: the negotiation of an agreement between a prosecutor and a defendant whereby the defendant is permitted to plead guilty to a reduced charge

—**plea-bargain** *intransitive verb*

—**plea bargain** *noun*

# "Quick & Dirty"
# Risks & Rewards

Whenever something is going to be used temporarily with little concern for quality, the "quick and dirty" approach may prove satisfactory. In fact, time constraints may make it imperative to do something "quick and dirty". Whatever the reasons for doing something "quick and dirty" you should keep in mind the potential risks and rewards. If you think that there is even a remote chance that you could suffer financially or mentally from pursuing a "quick and dirty" approach, you should abandon the project…hightail it, jump ship, get out of Dodge.

## Risks

There are three main risks associated with doing something "quick & dirty". The first and foremost risk is the "Mental" risk. Another risk is "Financial", and the third significant risk is "Reputation.

## Mental Risk

There is always the possibility of slipping into the mindset of doing things "quick & dirty" even when that is not the appropriate approach. If you have been successful with "quick & dirty", then doing things "quick

& dirty" perhaps has become second nature. It's easy for you to do things this way. That's not to say that you are incapable of doing things more refined and methodical, but doing things "quick & dirty" is preferable. The problem is that you become a "quick & dirty" machine, cranking things out routinely that are only marginally acceptable if at all. Others, most importantly your supervisors, lower their expectations for your work. You will see less and less stimulating and challenging assignments. Maybe this is OK with you. Maybe you work in a "quick & dirty" shop, where things are routinely done "quick & dirty". The hazard here is that it becomes more difficult to break away from that mindset, so when you are faced with an assignment that is not "quick & dirty", you struggle to meet the expectations and are less likely to be successful.

# Reputation risk

The risk that you will be known for doing things "quick & dirty" is one that should be contemplated seriously. A reputation for doing things "quick & dirty" may not be the reputation you want, not that things won't come your way, only the things that come your way may not be what you want. They will probably be things that were needed yesterday, putting enormous pressure on you. The choice, quality assignments are not likely to come your way, once you have been seen as having done something "quick & dirty". The word does get around. All is not lost, however. There is plenty of demand for "quick & dirty". The U.S. Government is ripe with those kinds of projects. Despite what you may have heard about the Government being slow about things, they are big time pursuers of "quick & dirty", based on my several years of experience, although mostly with the Department of Defense. I have heard the words "make it quick and dirty" numerous times.

# Financial risk

Whenever you undertake to do something "quick and dirty", you risk not being compensated adequately, or at all. As a matter of fact, you may be sued for not performing according to what was expected. If you sign a contract to do something and it does not specifically say in the contract that things are to be done "quick & dirty", and that is how you did things, you could be facing financial ruin and destitution.

# Rewards

Of course there are rewards associated with doing things "quick & dirty". These may be categorized as "Financial", "Reputation" and "Mental".

# Mental Rewards

If you are good at doing things "quick & dirty", then you probably get a sense of accomplishment more often than most, because you are successful at getting the things that need to be done in a hurry, done. I worked with a "quick & dirty" master for about five years who was very much appreciated by those for whom he did things "quick & dirty".

# Financial rewards

The financial rewards associated with doing things "quick & dirty" are difficult to calculate, but they can be huge. If say the U.S. Government gets in a crunch and needs something done "quick & dirty", as it often does, then it probably is willing to pay through the nose to get it accomplished. You should be charging megabucks for whatever when a U.S. Government Contracting Officer says he wants you to do something "quick & dirty". Actually, the Government does pay a premium for computer applications that are done "quick & dirty", it's called "Rapid Application Development" or RAD.

## Reputation rewards

Once you have successfully done something "quick & dirty" to someone else's satisfaction, you instantly will have become a "quick & dirty" guru. All kinds of "quick & dirty" projects will come your way. You don't have to advertise or prospect for business. You will be deluged with work. In fact you will have to turn down work there will be so much of it.

# Getting Talented
# "Quick & Dirty" People

Whenever any project is undertaken, it should be determined and communicated to everyone involved whether the project is to be done "quick & dirty". This will alarm those who do things precisely and methodically. They will find all kinds of excuses to be removed from the project, leaving you with the best "quick & dirty" talent available.

# Quick & Dirty Warnings

---

***WARNING***


Do not attempt to interrupt someone who is doing something "quick & dirty".  Quick bursts of anger with an abrupt barrage of foul language are likely. Once "quick & dirty has commenced, it must continue uninterrupted to its conclusion.

---

***WARNING***

Attempting to do something "quick & dirty" that should not be done that way likely will result in frustration, despair, lamentation and perhaps rejection.

***WARNING***

While watching someone gifted in the art of "quick & dirty" is a thing of beauty, watching someone struggling with "quick & dirty" can be horrifying, with arms and legs flailing away and wretched looks from the participant.

***WARNING***

If you are constantly doing things hastily with little concern for keeping things neat and clean, you could be suffering from *Chronic Quick & Dirty Mentality Disorder*, more commonly known as CQDMD. It is a common affliction in highly advanced societies where people have a dire need to do more in less time. Golf can help reduce or eliminate the problem entirely depending on how often you can tee it up. You must be exacting and methodical, and keep your equipment clean to do any good in golf. Quick & dirty just doesn't cut it in golf

# Rhymes
# &
# Poetry

When in doubt, leave it out!

Get on the ball, or you may stall!

Stay on track, there's no turning back!

Put it in overdrive, or you may not survive!

No time for a McFlurry, everyone's in a hurry!

Don't try thinking of a rhyme, there isn't time!


Quick & dirty could be just for you
Especially if you don't have a clue.

If quick & dirty is for you
This is what you should do

The "Quick and Dirty" Official Quick and Dirty Handbook

Don't think about the time of day
There's no time to play

Don't bother with a list of things to do
You don't have time to tie your shoe

Don't ask for directions
You're not concerned about corrections

Don't wonder what's for lunch
Nothing! We're in a crunch

Don't even take time to think
You barely have time to blink

There's no time to show you how
Just get to it, Now!

# Tips & Dead Giveaways

## For Identifying thing done Quick & Dirty

If you haven't seen the results of something that's been done "quick & dirty", the following tips and dead giveaways will help you. If you do most everything "quick & dirty" yourself, probably everything that you see that's been done "quick & dirty" looks OK to you. You are already aware of what to look for, although you just gloss over most everything anyway.

## Tips:

If there are misspellings, it's likely that it was done "quick & dirty".

If there are wholesale things missing, it's likely that it was done "quick & dirty".

If thoughts are not fully carried out, it's likely that it was done "quick & dirty".

## Dead Giveaways:

The table of contents doesn't follow what is in the document.

The page numbering is out of order.

Things are not lined up properly.

# Where to Get Help
# when you have been "quick & dirtied"

There are probably countless companies that could help you out from having been "quick and dirtied". The three firms listed below are ones that I am personally aware of that have significant successful experience in taking things that were done "quick & dirty" to where they should be. Some, I suspect, have gone directly to the garbage can.

MR Consulting, Inc.
Centreville, Virginia
703-830-6637

Syllogistic Solutions, Inc.
Springfield, Virginia
703-941-2009

TransData, LLC
Perry Hall, Maryland
410-529-0009

# Anti "Quick & Dirty" Culture

There is actually an anti "quick & dirty" culture thriving in the United States, the Amish. They decided a long time ago that they would have nothing to do with "quick & dirty". It is actually in their covenants. It says "anyone caught doing something "qucik & dirty" will be dragged by a donkey through a field of freshly laid manure. After reading this book, if you want to avoid "quick & dirty" altogether, you too may want to join them.

# Outlook

There will always be the need for "quick & dirty" talented people as long as there are deadlines, and as long as the U.S. Government continues to need things done yesterday, which is never-ending. Should this book become required reading for new business hires and "quick & dirty" is taught in colleges and trade schools, then the future is indeed bright for people with sound "quick & dirty" skills. As a matter of fact, it is highly likely that there will be a "quick & dirty" association, if there isn't already one. Maybe there will even be a "Quick & Dirty Institute of America". You may even see "quick & dirty" certifications.

## Missing and Closing

Things that were done "quick & dirty" usually have a lot of things that were left out or not fully finished. The remaining blank pages in this book represent those things that were left out of this "quick & dirty" book. Although in "quick & dirty, what was left out usually represents more than actually went into what was done "quick & dirty" there are not as many blank pages due to printing cost considerations and not to have you think it less appealing.

The blank pages may come in handy though where you work to make notes on your company's policy regarding doing things "quick & dirty". If they don't have one, they probably will after reading this book.

This book focuses on the implications of doing things "quick & dirty". Included are "to do's" and "not to do's", warning messages, examples of "quick & dirty", and exercises and fitness for "quick & dirty" work. It also establishes guidelines and identifies the risks and rewards of doing things "quick & dirty".

G. Robert Michaelis developed numerous database applications that were identified and assigned as "quick & dirty" projects. He worked with "quick & dirty" masters who routinely cranked out applications in a matter of a few hours. His several years of experience in environments fraught with the "quick & dirty" mentality enabled him to accumulate a vast amount of knowledge on the practice of doing things "quick & dirty". He does not profess, however, to be a "quick & dirty" pro. He does have the uncanny ability though of being able to identify work that was performed "quick & dirty", particularly database applications.

**This book was written to help you do things "quick & dirty" when you need to, and that occurs more often than you may think.**

www.ingramcontent.com/pod-product-compliance
Lightning Source LLC
Chambersburg PA
CBHW021545200526
45163CB00015B/1624